When In Doubt Lead...

Part 2

The Leaders Guide to Personal and Organizational Development in the Fire Service

by
Dennis Compton

Published by
Fire Protection Publications
Oklahoma State University
2000

ISBN 0-87939-179-0
Library of Congress #00-103240

First Edition
First Printing, May 2000
Printed in the United States of America

Contact us for more information about Fire Protection Publications at Oklahoma State University, headquarters of International Fire Service Training Association:

Send email to *editors@istafpp.okstate.edu*
Phone (405) 744-5723
Write to 930 North Willis, OSU, Stillwater, OK 74078
Or see our web page at *www.ifsta.org.*

Contents

Dedication

The International Fire Service Training Association (IFSTA) has been the primary provider of validated training manuals and other materials to the fire service for almost seven decades. It is my pleasure to have been an active IFSTA participant for over twenty years.

This book is dedicated to past, present, and future IFSTA Delegates and Staff who unselfishly give their time and energy to provide a safe country by ensuring a more effective fire service.

Introduction

Leadership manifests itself within an organization in a variety of ways. . . from inside and outside the system. This book is designed around some unique aspects of fire service leadership. Each has a significant impact on the overall effectiveness of the people in the organization and their collective standing in the community. The areas addressed include personal leadership characteristics; organizational ethics; managing career development in order to enhance performance and build succession capability; guidelines for creating and institutionalizing organizational and programmatic change; and developing and nurturing relationships in the community and neighborhoods.

As we know, nothing exists in isolation. Within an organization, everything is in some way connected to everything else. The areas covered in this book certainly reflect this relationship. Consider the following concepts:

- As we lead others, our effectiveness will be regulated, to a degree, by our ability to lead ourselves.

- It is difficult to maintain a positive, productive, and healthy work environment without a strong ethical foundation to guide the behavior of all members, irrespective of their rank or role.

- An organization cannot outperform its commitment to the growth of its members. There are individual and organizational requirements, that if not addressed, make it almost impossible to develop an environment committed to excellence and able to shift organizational emphasis or change direction.

- In the work-world of today, fire departments and other organizations that cannot demonstrate progressive, meaningful, and measurable efforts to change and improve will experience considerably more internal and external scrutiny. The better we understand the basic change elements that leaders can use, the more effective change efforts will be. Just like everything else, change must be managed to be successful.

- The fire service must stay connected to its customers if our standing in society is to remain positive (and even continue to improve). Fire stations play a key role in this process. They reside in every neighborhood, in every community. No other service delivery group can compete with a fire department's ability to connect and influence the people they serve. This connection and influence can only improve performance in programs like public education and within other programs and components of the mission.

The importance of understanding the interrelatedness of these (and other) organizational responsibilities cannot be over-stated. This book is intended to discuss each area and help readers make the appropriate connections within their own work environment and situation. I hope it accomplishes that goal, and that you find it simple, useful, and thought provoking.

2

Personal Leadership. . . A Key to Our Future

Most of us begin our fire service careers with a fire burning in our bellies and with the intent of being around for a long time. The challenges of day-to-day life at home and at work confront all of us and sometimes make it difficult to keep that fire from dimming over the years. We have all known people in the fire service who were as positive and fulfilled at the end of their careers as they were in the very beginning. We have also known people who, for a variety of reasons, were not. They may have become disenchanted with the work they were doing or the changes in the fire service since they started. They may have become unhappy with their department, their bosses, co-workers, and sometimes even their friends and family. It is difficult for other team members when a co-worker demonstrates this behavior, but it can be paralyzing to a team when a leader displays this behavior. The demeanor of leaders and their outlook in general have a tremendous impact on the workers and the mission. Working with a specific person can be the best or worst thing that can happen in someone's career, and the impact (either way) can be long-lasting.

Although there is no magic formula, people from different parts of the country and different areas of the fire service have shared specific suggestions for staying positive, productive, and healthy. These traits and behaviors can be contagious to others and help maintain the passion that initially attracted us to the fire service. The following represents some of their collective thoughts:

- Diet and exercise have always been key elements of physical, emotional, and psychological wellness. These become even more important because of the hectic schedules we now keep in our lives.

- We should establish strong personal and professional values. In the fire service business, composure should be one of our core values. Remember that we lead primarily by example.

- At times, we all face tests of our confidence. It's during those times that we must go forward and move past our apprehensions.

- Hope is a key component within our sense of well being. Try not to give up or quit while experiencing a low period.

- Self-discipline moves us towards our goals in life.

- Planning sets our direction, tells us where we're going, and improves our confidence and the confidence of those around us.

- Be careful when choosing who you want to be like. . . you might get your wish.

- We all know that money isn't everything. There are many things in life that no amount of money can buy. Identify and cherish them.

- An element of success is the ability to sell yourself and your vision of the future. These must be sold in several different directions on a regular basis.

4

- In today's workplace, we must be able to form and lead outstanding teams, as well as perform effectively as a team member ourselves.

- Think and act as though people are our most important resource and remember that relationships drive people's effectiveness to a large extent. Help others deal with change.

- Find a great mentor and become one for someone else. Give freely to others and you will feel enriched yourself.

- Embrace and model accountability and the acceptance of responsibility. There are times when somebody needs to be "sweating the details."

- When in doubt, do the "right thing" in a given situation. This is usually what is best for you, others, and the organization as a whole.

- Develop exceptional communications skills. Never stop learning and never stop listening to others.

- There is no substitute for staying competent in our chosen field.

- Bad things happen to everyone. The difference is how we handle these difficult times and whether we rebound from them.

Additional Thoughts for Leaders

- Leaders should strive to approach their current duties with the same teamwork-based attitude that they naturally utilized from the beginning of their fire service careers.

5

Maintaining a sense of self-motivation that is directed toward competence, safety, learning, teaching, and overall wellness is very important.

- Being consistent and predictable helps others interact positively with leaders and helps leaders maintain their own sense of direction. Trying to be as fair as possible, avoiding the appearance of favoritism, displaying trust in people, being honest in our interactions with others, and simply being nice to people can serve as daily "booster shots" to a person's sense of self-worth and organizational value.

- Being a good coach and working on communications skills can help avoid personnel problems that can begin to get us down as leaders. Confronting issues in a productive way is preferred rather than letting them fester until emotions get the best of us—sometimes resulting in negative, long lasting reactions among those who were involved.

- As much as possible, stay focused on the mission, committed to service delivery, and concerned about the welfare of co-workers. Supporting the organization, buying into the future, and setting a positive example can be contagious when modeled by the leader.

- Approaching situations with the same flexibility, eagerness, and empathy that we displayed early in our careers can help keep our spirits high. Encouraging participation and input helps to create an environment in which the work is taken seriously, yet the workers are able to have fun doing it. A positive work environment builds and nurtures positive, productive people.

- Bad things that happen at home should not dominate the work environment, and difficult times at work should not create barriers to family relationships at home. That concept is much easier to write than it is to do, but if we consider its importance periodically, we will probably manage this balance better than if we pay no attention to it at all.

The Five L's

Many years ago, a sports psychologist and friend named Gary Mack shared with me a five-part prescription for long-term physical, psychological, and emotional well being, which I have passed along to others over the years. It is important that we give attention to our own sense of well being so that we can be ready to consistently do the set of things necessary in our jobs and personal lives. It might be helpful to share these Five L's:

- ***Love:*** Love is an essential element of a person's feeling of self-worth and well being. It is important that we have love in our lives and are able to enjoy and appreciate the positive emotions we feel for and receive from family, friends, pets, activities, etc. Placing a priority on these relationships and enjoyments can provide a healthy balance in our lives.

- ***Learn:*** People who have stopped learning, or have the sense that they are "fully trained," are on a downhill slide in their careers. In fact, in the emergency services business, they are dangerous to themselves and others. Always pay attention, learn from experience, continue training and education, and keep an open mind to change and improvement. We should never stop learning at any point in your careers...or in your lives.

7

- **Labor:** Work is good for the soul. Many times it provides a feeling of accomplishment and self-worth that no other aspect of our lives can offer. If we can find something we enjoy doing, do it well, develop pride in its value to others, and embrace the challenge that it provides to us; our work can be an important part of overall wellness. It is said that when a person stops doing meaningful work, a part of them dies.

- **Laugh:** A positive (not hurtful) sense of humor is important and can offset the effects of stress. It keeps us from taking our roles and ourselves so seriously that we become obsessed or ineffective. Laughter is good medicine, and a few doses every day can extend our careers, and maybe our lives.

- **Leave:** Eventually, everyone leaves. Most people who are at the end of enjoyable careers say that they simply don't know where the time went. When that time has come, and for whatever reason, it is time to leave, let's hope we leave something behind that will continue on for others. Significant contributions tend to be lasting, but we cannot wait until the end of our careers to decide to offer or accomplish them. It could be too late. Contributions that endure are usually built one step at a time over a significant period of time. Leaving something behind for the future should be an ongoing effort and goal for each of us.

I really do not know how, where, or from whom these five words of guidance originated, but I know that they can help us stay on course and are worth a few minutes of thought now and then.

8

Conclusion

Managing, delivering, or supporting a full range of fire and life safety services requires a great deal of skill and knowledge, but it also requires considerable commitment and leadership. Maintaining oneself as a positive, productive, and healthy contributor to the system, over the long haul, presents one of the most difficult and important challenges in our careers. We know that management skills and leadership traits are interrelated, and without adequate doses of both, sustaining successful performance is not possible.

We are all subject to up and down cycles at work and at home. A valid question is "Are there specific, realistic behaviors and concepts that we can practice to help us stay positive, productive, and healthy contributors for the entire duration of our careers?" I know many leaders who do this very well and have been a great influence on the careers of others. They have found a way to keep their fires burning, which can help sustain or re-ignite the fire in others. We all know that this can have a positive affect on the mission and on the internal relationships among workers, as well. Since we are planning to be around for a long time, we may as well enjoy ourselves and help those around us do the same. It's up to us individually to find excitement, passion, fulfillment, and self-satisfaction in our work. Nobody can do that for us. If you are bored, figure out a way to liven things up and ignite your internal fire once again. This chapter does not contain a secret formula. The information has probably been around forever. I have never known anyone who could live up to each of these personal leadership characteristics and considerations all the time. I did not invent the concepts and behaviors in this chapter, but I admire people I've known

9

who try hard everyday to practice them. They are positive, productive, and healthy most days, and so are most of the people around them. We cannot expect to lead others effectively if we cannot provide positive leadership to ourselves. It will not happen by chance, so we should pay some attention to the concept of "personal leadership" on a regular basis.

An Expanded View of Ethics 2

The subject of business ethics has always seemed straightforward to me. In contemplating the subject of ethical behavior, I think about various agreements we make (whether we know it or not) when we accept our positions in the fire service. Ethical behavior seems to revolve around a set of personal and organizational responsibilities and commitments. We meet these responsibilities and commitments through verbal and/or written "ethical contracts" we enter into when we become firefighters, inspectors, public educators, chiefs, or other positions or roles within our organizations. As we consider the concept of ethics within a broader perspective, we develop a roadmap that could serve to guide us on a day-to-day, person-to-person, situational basis. Nobody can live up to the expectations outlined within this expanded ethics model every day. However, it tends to give each of us a goal to work toward, measure ourselves against, and use as a target at which to shoot. Doing so is difficult when one considers all of the variables that effect our daily behavior and how many different people judge and evaluate us, often from different perspectives. Exploring this expanded concept of ethics has been interesting, and I would like to share with you a unique perspective on the subject.

The ethical contracts to which we commit ourselves cover specific responsibilities within five areas:

- External customers

- Internal customers

- Leadership and followership

- Professional conduct

- Personal commitment

Each of these areas has its own unique set of success elements.

External Customers

The first area we will explore deals with the ethical contract we enter into with our external customers. This contract is almost always unwritten but gets to the very heart of our existence as a service. In fact, if we were to tell our customers (up front) that we were not willing to buy into these responsibilities, I doubt they would allow us to serve in the positions of public trust that we hold (career or volunteer; line or support). Our compliance with these commitments is taken for granted by the people we serve. In essence, we tell our external customers that as members and leaders of their fire service we will:

- *Stay ready to respond quickly.* This is a basic expectation of fire departments. For example, we should keep ourselves (or our fire companies) in position to respond quickly within our first due response areas in order to consistently meet the emergency response goals of the mission. As another example, we should respond to EMS calls with the same sense of urgency that we do fire calls. Bottom line: one of the primary reasons we exist is to safely and effectively deliver a specific menu of services to our customers when called upon to do so. Prevention, public education, and emergency response are primary responsibilities. Everything else should be geared to support these three service delivery responsibilities.

12

- *Be trained and equipped to perform the job.* It is our responsibility to attain levels of competency through training and to be able to use the equipment provided in order to perform effectively.

- *Care about our customers and their property.* The concepts of customer service and loss control provide significant anchor points for these efforts—no matter what service we are providing. In most cases, our customers judge us more from the impressions we leave rather than the details of performing specific tasks. The fire service displays its caring approach daily, and it serves us well. This approach should be the foundation for delivering prevention, public education, and emergency services to our customers.

- *Exist to serve, not to overindulge ourselves in our own creature comforts.* We should always keep in mind our primary role, which is to deliver service, even if at times that role results in our own comfort levels being disrupted. Some of what we do today is a form of social or public service responses, but we are also in the life-and-death business. We do not get to pick the time of the day that those critical situations will occur. We must always be ready to deliver the appropriate type and level of service required in any given situation. We are in place to prevent harm, educate the public to avoid or survive a variety of dangerous events, respond to emergencies when called upon to do so, and operate a full range of support systems to ensure fire departments are capable of providing service to our external customers.

- *Provide excellent service at a competitive price.* Our customers want value for their dollars, just as we do. When we are at their homes, schools, businesses, etc., they really do not care how we did on our last fire, heart attack, or public education class. At that point in time they are primarily interested in how well we perform with their situation. That is a high standard of excellence to which to be held, but our services are of great value to our customers.

- *Use our skills to help the customer at every opportunity and maximize the importance of our customer's needs.* Treat every encounter and incident as if it is important to us, even though our life-saving medical skills, fire fighting, or other technical skills may not be necessary to deliver the service or resolve the problem. Giving the impression that the customer's problem is not important enough to have called upon us can be perceived as arrogance. In my career, I don't know of a person who has called us for emergency services who was not having a bad day. In fact, when they think back on the day they had to call the fire department, they may remember it as one of the worst days of their lives.

- *Prevent emergencies from occurring whenever and however we can.* We should devote our resources to not only preventing fires in our communities, but also to delivering all risk public education programs. All risk public education must be an active, integrated program in fire departments and within communities.

- *Be honest about what the department is staffed, equipped, and deployed to do, and what it cannot accomplish due to a lack of staffing, equipment, or other related issues.* We are the ones who should help the policy makers and the public make informed decisions about matters relating to emergency and non-emergency service levels. That is not an easy task for us to accomplish. It requires evaluation of our capabilities and continual communication and education.

14

These represent some of the individual and organizational expectations and behaviors that form the basis of the ethical contract with external customers. These are timeless in their importance to our customers and define the basic commitment we made to them when we assumed the responsibilities of the positions we hold. We made an agreement with our customers and they expect us to keep it every day.

Internal Customers

The next area identifies the elements of our ethical contract relating to our internal customers (each other). If we as workers or supervisors used or abused our physical resources (like trucks, stations, or equipment) in a way that diminished their value and/or jeopardized their future usefulness to the department, we would be held accountable for our actions and perhaps even punished. However, human resources are sometimes abused and misused, and our leaders do not say a word about it. When this occurs, it is not in the best interest of service delivery or our workforce.

There are some basic behaviors that define the key elements of this typically unwritten ethical contract that we share with each other and with fire service members in general. In addressing them, we should:

- *Be considerate of others' feelings and property at work and practice discretion in the things we say and do to each other.*

- *Accept the differences in us and respect the opportunities that diversity offers.* There is nothing wrong with being black, white, brown, male, female, Protestant, Catholic, Jewish, sworn, civilian, staff, line, etc. These are simply some of the

15

differences among us. When brought together, these differences provide a clearer focus and usually result in better decisions as a group. These differences also form the general makeup of our external customer base. Their perspective will always provide enhanced guidance to achieve more effective service delivery programs.

- *Emphasize the importance of unity in the organization in good times and in bad times.* Relationships are not usually evaluated when things are going well. They are primarily judged on how the system and the individuals act and react when things are not going well. That becomes the true measure of organizational unity and collective strength. How do the people in the system act toward each other when something is wrong?

- *Require members to be involved in their jobs and participate in improvement efforts, at least in areas that directly impact their performance.* This should not be optional for members of the organization. As long as we are members, we should be committed to performing and improving in the roles and jobs that we are assigned.

- *Stress the importance of change and keep the department moving forward.* It is the responsibility of leaders to keep an eye toward tomorrow and help the members of the department move in that direction.

- *Be thankful and humble about what we have—we shouldn't take good times in the organization for granted.* We are fortunate to have the personal and professional benefits that accompany our affiliation with the fire service. Forgetting this can start a journey towards personal and/or organizational problems with our work and our overall sense of direction.

16

- *Do all we can to help our members survive their careers.* The safety and survival of our workers are the most critical measurements of organizational wellness in a fire department. Senior members are somewhat responsible for helping the junior members live long enough to become senior. That is how it has always been and probably always will be. If we hold positions of leadership, we have the responsibility for the safety of all members. Even so, all members have the responsibility for their own safety and the safety of each other, irrespective of the position they hold. Establishing, teaching, and enforcing safety policies and procedures are not always popular, but are always necessary.

- *Favoritism should not play a role in work-related decisions.* This can be a very difficult issue for the fire service because of the many long-term relationships and friendships we form over the years. As we move into supervisory positions, favoritism can easily become a problem. It is a good practice to periodically review this issue in our hearts and minds, and in our supervisory practices as well.

These behaviors and expectations form the elements of the unwritten ethical contract we have with our members—our internal customers. A lack of attention to these issues can damage relationships, reduce effectiveness, compromise the mission, and make working with each other difficult, at best.

Leadership/Followership

The next ethical contract is entered into when we accept positions of leadership within our departments. However, leaders in one setting (formal or informal) are almost always followers in another, and visa versa. Therefore, this contract

17

pertains directly to each of us. The following are ethical behaviors that are important to being effective leaders and followers:

- *Tell people up front what is expected of them.* When asked to identify the most important things they need and expect from a supervisor, workers have always said "tell me what is expected of me." Yet this critical expectation of leadership is many times avoided and therefore results in unnecessary conflict.

- *Treat isolated mistakes as just that. . . **isolated** mistakes.* It is an organizational fact that if the price of failure is not acceptable to the workers, they will initiate only minor, "safe" changes involving minimal risk to them as the change agents. Managing failure is an important element of change or idea management.

- *Reward good performance and behavior at every opportunity, but do not ever reward unacceptable performance or bad behavior.* People tend to repeat behavior that is rewarded. Hold positive acts up in the organization for all to see as examples of what is expected from all members.

- *When things get worse, we need to get better.* This should become an organizational value in the fire service simply because of the emergency nature of much of our business. As emergency responders, we inherit situations that are sometimes absolutely out of control. Self-control is a skill that can be taught, learned, and thus improved upon. We should constantly, throughout our careers, try to improve in this area. A great deal of respect comes to fire service leaders that are at their best when the situation is at its worst. When the leader is coming apart, the rest of the participants are not far behind. These are difficult skills to master, but ones we should all work to develop.

18

- *Stress self-discipline, but be willing and able to impose corrective, progressive, and lawful discipline when self-discipline breaks down.* This is one of the cornerstones of a positive, productive, and healthy organization.

- *Develop tomorrow's leaders.* We owe this to our departments and to those individuals coming through the system. The long-term success of an organization is directly related to the on-going investment made in those who will lead it in the future. Succession planning and career development are key program elements of this effort.

- *Don't forget what the department was formed to do or from where we came.* Bottom line: the fire department exists to deliver service; it is not intended or funded to service our egos and personal agendas. No matter what else is going on in the fire service, nothing is more important than being able to prevent emergencies, educate the customers, or deliver emergency service effectively as a team every time we are called upon to do so. If it were our own house on fire, or our loved ones trapped in a vehicle, that is exactly what we would expect. We would accept nothing less.

- *Do not do things to our supervisors that we would not want done to us.* We should do all we can to help those around us be successful in their roles—including our bosses.

- *Avoid the ready-fire-aim approach to problem-solving and decision-making.* Get the information and facts needed before beginning a course of action. Acting on incorrect or incomplete information is a sure way to achieve poor performance.

- *Work to resolve conflict, and do not be a consistent obstacle to doing so in the department.* Conflict is important to the

19

change process, but unresolved conflict can become a very negative influence in the system. Sometimes it seems to be the same people who get in the way of progress no matter what the issue. Try not to fill this role.

- *Leave the system better than we found it in some way—no matter what positions we may hold in the department.* Leaving something behind for the future is a goal that we should all work toward during our careers.

The elements of the ethical Contact we enter into as leaders and followers are important no matter what role we play in the department. The commitment we make to this effort affects not only ourselves, but many others with whom we interact (or lead) on a regular basis.

Professional Conduct

The next ethical contract relates to our professional conduct. For many of us, this is the first thing that comes to mind when someone mentions the word "ethics." The following are some key elements of this ethical contract:

- *All of the Boy and Girl Scout things we learned as kids continue to be important in our work life and personal life. . . forever.* These formed the basis of socially acceptable behavior in our early development and are a great foundation from which to continue to operate as adults.

- *Manage politics in a way that does not cause the organization to suffer significantly for someone's own temporary or personal gain.* The well being of the organization and the needs of the external customers should come first, ahead of any individual's gain inside the department.

- *We must operate within the law and manage finances appropriately.* This gets to the heart of public trust in a public official. We can go to jail for not doing this.

- *Attempt to operate within the philosophy, culture, and values of the organization.* Even if the culture is in need of significant change, do not display an overall disrespect for the members and their role in the lives of others. Also, do not display an open disrespect for past accomplishments and efforts. These actions could render a leader professionally and operationally impotent within the department. Cultural change can be important to organizational growth and is most successfully led (over time) from the inside of that culture and value system.

- *Giving our word or making a deal must mean something.* When it doesn't, people won't trust or respect us. Without trust and respect, professional work relationships are impossible to develop and nurture. This directly impacts our overall effectiveness as individuals and collectively as members of an organization.

The elements of the ethical contract outlining our professional conduct are important pieces of the overall ethical picture. Some parts of this agreement may actually be covered in written form. They are important to everyone we come in contact with at work.

Personal Commitment

The fifth and final ethical contract is the one we make to ourselves and relates to our own personal commitment and well being. It is just as important as the others because it defines our

21

character and commitment to our work, and perhaps even the life we have chosen to live. The elements of this ethical contract are as follows:

- *Begin each day with the assumption that we can make a positive difference in the lives that we contact.* This approach has a significant impact on our self-esteem, as well as our overall emotional and psychological health.

- *Only make promises that can most likely be kept.* This becomes a key element of integrity. One's word is possibly their most prized possession.

- *Do not lie, steal, or get involved in conflicts of interest with our work.* These are basic behaviors that form the right-of-passage to the rest of the ethical issues discussed in this chapter. Struggling with any of these creates substantial ethical and relationship problems.

- *Avoid being self-righteous about our personal values and beliefs.* Self-righteousness hinders the ability to lead others and sometimes sends the message that we place ourselves morally above others. This behavior separates the workforce into two groups: The Good People and the Bad People. The problem then is that the Good People always get to decide who the Bad People are. This can destroy any sense of organizational unity.

- *Model the behaviors that are expected from others.* Quite simply, personal character is judged by what we actually do rather than what we say we're going to do. If we expect those we lead to display certain characteristics, traits and behaviors, then we must try to model those ourselves. This forms the foundation for leading-by-example, which has been a key success element for leadership longer than any of us have been around.

22

- *Maintain a balance among those things that are important to us in life, and remember that those things are different for different people.* We may be firefighters, public educators, inspectors, clerks, mechanics, fathers, mothers, sons, daughters, husbands, wives, friends, coaches, social leaders, church leaders, teachers, or a myriad of other roles. These various roles can provide personal balance and prevent us from solely identifying with any one aspect, role, or person in our life. It becomes more difficult to be completely devastated by losing any one piece of our life when we wear several different hats and understand the importance of each to our overall sense of balance and well being.

- *Be nice to other people.* It doesn't cost anything and dramatically improves every aspect of our lives and the lives of those around us.

- *Value friends and family and be careful not to take them for granted. They can easily (and quickly) be gone. . .* Enough said!

- *Admit when you have made a mistake.* Take responsibility for your mistake, develop a plan to correct it, try to prevent it from happening again, and go on.

- *We shouldn't take ourselves (or our roles) so seriously that we are no longer effective.* A good friend has told me many times not to let the ego rise above the heart, and this has been good advice over the years. Think about the long-term effectiveness of those who feel they cannot be replaced or feel that the entire success of the organization or workgroup rests solely on their shoulders every day. This is not usually a good situation and almost always results in an ugly outcome.

- *Strive to identify (to yourself) the things for which you stand.* Hopefully this will not be a long list. It can be helpful to ask yourself, "What is special about working for/with me?" There should be something that you can identify that is important to you as a leader and as a person. This is what defines those few, but important lines that you draw, move others toward, and react around.

The ethical contract that we make to ourselves and our personal commitment to that contract help us keep our perspective, and to a large extent, help us maintain self-esteem and our sense of well-being. We cannot be of service to others unless we can do what it takes to sustain ourselves as positive, productive, and healthy contributors.

Conclusion

These five ethical contracts are intended to paint a more complete picture of ethics in general. I've never met a person who measures up to these ethical standards every day, but I have met those who were trying to do so on a regular basis. This chapter is not theory. The content identifies specific ethical behaviors and expectations for all members of fire service organizations. Each element of the five contracts is so interrelated that I do not know where one might begin to eliminate the components. These components determine how our behavior is judged inside the system, outside the system, by those with whom we work directly, and even by ourselves. If we are going to shoot at an ethical target, let's try for a difficult one. Anything that hits even close to the center of this more challenging target will produce better results than ten bulls-eyes on an easier target. I guess we should all reflect periodically on the attention we give to each of these five ethical contracts. Who knows, it might make us more effective in whatever role(s) we play—both at work and at home.

24

Program-Based Career Management... An Organizational and Individual Guide

The management of a person's career is a difficult challenge and responsibility for the organization and the individual. We hire people at relatively young ages, benefit from their minds, hearts, and bodies for the majority of their adult work lives, then send them off to retirement. Trying to be all things to all people almost always produces negative organizational results. However having a better understanding of the personal and professional needs of our work force throughout their careers and into their retirement, and then providing a guide for them to follow as they take this journey makes sense and is good human resource management. This chapter will define the program elements that comprise this guide.

Most organizations have a thorough plan for managing their fleet of vehicles. They know when each was purchased; what preventative and regular maintenance will be required (and its frequency); what special maintenance might be needed based on specific uses of the vehicle; a record of significant breakdowns that have occurred; and of course, the year the vehicle will be surplused (if at all); and the condition it might be in when it is no longer retained. We are overdue in providing similar guidance for managing our human resources as well. This guidance should include programs designed around the physical, emotional, and psychological needs of our workforce. It should also include a program-based system for helping people be positive, productive, contributing members throughout their careers. Bottom line: the organization's efforts should revolve around providing the highest quality of service or product possible outside the system, while also providing the best support possible to its members.

For purposes of discussion, a career can be broken down into three separate (yet overlapping) periods. They include:

1. Selection and Entry

2. The Career Journey

3. Transition to Retirement

Each of these periods of a career has its own set of success measurements. The measurements form the basis of major program areas that contribute to the overall effectiveness of career management. The more effectively these programs are managed, the more consistent the overall human resource management effort will be. Thus, the more effectively workers perform. In order to assist in evaluating the current state of your organization's performance, let's further define each component period and its program elements.

Selection and Entry

This period is critical because it attempts to match the candidate with the job. Once selected, its the time when the new employees are oriented to the organization. The goal is to do so in a way that builds a strong foundation for a positive, productive employment relationship.

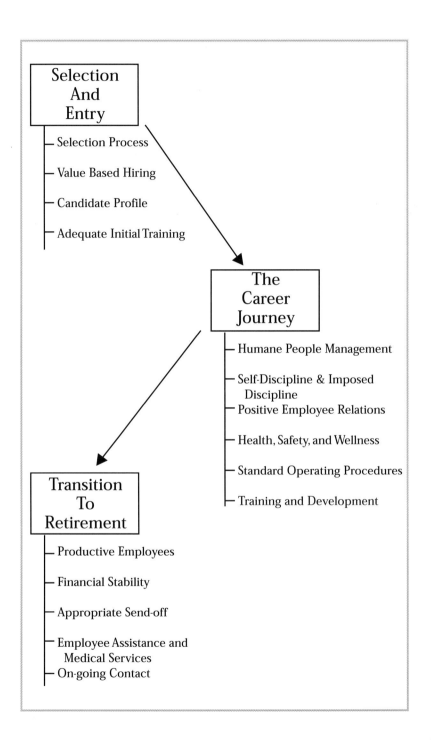

Selection
And
Entry

— Selection Process

— Value Based Hiring

— Candidate Profile

— Adequate Initial Training

The
Career
Journey

— Humane People Management

— Self-Discipline & Imposed
  Discipline
— Positive Employee Relations

— Health, Safety, and Wellness

— Standard Operating Procedures

— Training and Development

Transition
To
Retirement

— Productive Employees

— Financial Stability

— Appropriate Send-off

— Employee Assistance and
  Medical Services
— On-going Contact

27

- **Selection Process:** A fair, open, and valid selection process is an important beginning to a candidate's contact with the organization. We should seek candidates who are qualified and who add diversity to a work force that is representative of our customer base. A process that does not discriminate on any basis other than job-related and valid performance criteria is an important element in organizational integrity. Whether selected or not, the process that the candidate goes through must provide equal access for all who apply. For those candidates who are interested, support and assistance can be made available. This need not be a spoon-feeding exercise, but rather take the form of career counseling and guidance . . . and perhaps even mentoring. Steering candidates toward additional education or experiential learning can be critical to their overall preparation and subsequent performance on the job.

- **Value-Based Hiring:** Successful candidates should possess certain traits and characteristics that will have an on-going positive effect on their short- and long-term performance in the organization. This starts with selecting candidates who possess positive perceptions of the organization and whose values match those of the organization. Why hire an individual who already has a negative opinion of the organization or whose values are out of balance with the organization itself? Successful candidates should demonstrate a sincere, realistic appreciation for the organization and a clear picture of what their role will be. Hiring a 1990-model candidate in the year 2000 is asking for trouble with job satisfaction and performance down the road. The fact is, jobs change, and they will continue to change. A willingness (and ability) to accept this reality will result in more positive, productive, and satisfied employees and supervisors in the future.

28

Sample of Desired Characteristics and Values in Job Candidates

- Physically capable of performing required manipulative skills

- Self-motivated and dependable

- Honest

- Having self-respect/self-esteem/confidence (yet a degree of humility)

- Respectful of others

- Having a desire to serve others/service oriented

- Team player

- Empathetic and compassionate

- Willing to change/flexible

- Loyal

- Willing to learn

- Assertive, when necessary

- Follows instructions

- Displays leadership capability

- Willing to make a decision

- Displays good judgement

- Commitment to the organization

- Career and goal oriented

- Displays effective social skills (inside and outside the organization)

- Concern for one's own safety

29

- Psychological and emotional fitness

- Can read and comprehend what must be learned in order to perform

- Innovative

- Displays a positive attitude

- Self-disciplined

- Sense of humor

- Pride in appearance

- Good communications skills (written and verbal)

- Respects diversity and values other people

- **Candidate Profile:** As I have already said, organizations should identify characteristics that tend to profile successful employees and use the profile to help evaluate candidates. This is not (and should not be) an attempt to clone the people that we hire. After all, one organizational strength is diversity. However, there are some things that successful candidates must possess and build upon throughout their careers. These, coupled with adequate and current initial training, can set the stage for the success over the long run.

Frankly, organizations get some candidates who are not suited for a career with them. If these candidates are hired, no amount of training will overcome the fact that the organization made a hiring error. Over time, mismatched employees can become negative influences that spread their dissatisfaction through the department. This will effect the organization's performance. The elements that revolve around employee selection are critical to the overall effectiveness of the organization, and will effect the overall organizational health, today and in the future.

30

- **Adequate Initial Training:** Employees need a clear definition of their duties and role in the organization. People cannot be expected to perform well when they are not sure what is expected of them.

The Career Journey

After a person is selected and hired, there are many issues that require attention throughout the person's career. Leaving this process to chance creates a role-of-the-dice approach to maintaining our human resources as they deliver our services or products to the internal and external customers. Some of these areas of emphasis might include:

- **Humane People Management:** A cornerstone of organizational and individual effectiveness lies in a policy that requires a sensible and humane approach to everyday people management. A work environment that cannot (or will not) address this difficult issue should not expect to foster an environment that reflects an emotionally and psychologically fit workforce. It is not practical or realistic to expect members to treat external customers like queens and kings when they themselves are treated like unimportant, replaceable commodities inside the organization. We all know, and have witnessed, the effect of poor supervisory and leadership practices on the members of an organization. It is safe to say that our workers will not treat external customers better than the members of the organization are treated by each other (internally) on a day-to-day basis. As experts tell us, abused children often become child abusers.

There should be no tolerance for supervisory actions that are abusive towards the members. One way to begin to counter

31

these types of problems is for the members of a department to commit the time and effort necessary to document the culture, philosophy, and values of the organization. Once compiled, publish them and refer to them regularly. This document could include individual roles, organizational expectations, and the expectations of supervisors and leaders. Creating such a document will represent a long-term investment in the internal environment of the organization.

- **Self-Discipline and Imposed Discipline:** Self-discipline forms the foundation of a progressive disciplinary policy that is centered around preventing performance problems and correcting behavior that is out of balance. Self-discipline not only relates to voluntary compliance with performance and behavior standards, but also with maintaining some sense of balance between family (or personal) responsibilities and work related responsibilities. When either is significantly disturbed, it almost always affects the other. An important piece of self-discipline lies in a periodic evaluation of our personal and professional well being. It is a delicate balance, but paying attention to our behavior at home and at work, on a regular basis, is one of the indicators of a healthy person. Healthy people in groups, add up to a healthy organization.

  It is important that imposed disciplinary action occurs in a positive, progressive, corrective, and lawful manner within the organization. Imposed discipline should include consideration for the future well being of the member(s) involved. Sometimes people's re-entry into the work environment and the periodic follow-up of their behavior can be critical to the long-term effectiveness of the disciplinary action that was taken.

32

- **Positive Employee Relations:** The environment in which we work sets the stage for collective and individual success. Positive employee relations are a critical piece of that success in any workforce. In an organization with a unionized workforce, it is almost impossible to foster employee involvement, empowerment, participative planning, or a sense of commitment and ownership without developing a labor/ management relationship that is supportive and committed to this effort. This process involves more than simply negotiating an agreement relating to wages, hours, and benefits. It means stepping outside of our traditional, confrontational roles and embracing a more cooperative approach geared toward delivering exceptional service (or a great product) to external customers, while also providing exceptional support to our internal customers (the members of the organization). Developing common goals and learning how to disagree constructively while resolving conflict are skills that require trust, respect, commitment, and patience. The psychological wellness of the organization as a whole can be greatly enhanced by a constructive working relationship between labor and management. It boils down to an issue of leadership, that, perhaps more than any other element, enhances or diminishes the organization's ability to change, improve, and compete.

- **Health, Safety, and Wellness:** The commitment to health, safety, and wellness issues is a message that must be reinforced on a regular basis. Fitness programs, regular physicals, injury rehabilitation, and other elements of a total wellness package are programmatic goals that can be creatively met over time. With such a commitment, an organization can have a more complete wellness program tomorrow than they had yesterday. If heath and wellness is a "big deal" to the leadership of labor and management, it will, over time, become a big deal to the membership. Patience and creativity by the members are critical to the success of a long-range approach to building health and wellness programs.

Psychological, emotional, and spiritual support is important to any group of people that are in place to achieve a common goal or mission. This is a component of the wellness package that is usually addressed through Employee Assistance and/or Chaplaincy Programs. Whether your organization has implemented one or both (or neither), says a great deal about how the organization's leadership views the members. In many organizations, we hire people for the majority of their adult lives. A reasonable person would predict that during this time, these members might experience personal and/or professional challenges that require a helping hand to cope with or overcome them…much like everyone else in society. These support programs represent a worthwhile investment in our employees and pay tremendous dividends over time.

A recently developed concept is called "pre-briefing for success." It is grounded in the belief that members will tend to perform better when they are prepared from a skills and knowledge standpoint, but also prepared psychologically, emotionally, and spiritually for the more stressful events they will encounter. Pre-briefing for success provides a roadmap to minimizing the effects of psychological and emotional stress on members. It includes, in addition to other elements, on-going communications issues that should be addressed. It is very important that members have a clear understanding of what is expected of them and what their role in the overall work process is expected to be.

This understanding begins to define those things for which we should hold ourselves responsible and those things for which we should not. Regular discussions about these and other issues and individual contact and follow-up by supervisors, are very important "pre-briefing" considerations. Pre-briefing for success might help to minimize the physical, psychological, emotional, and spiritual effects of stress that a person might encounter in their life. The pre-briefing process is not intended to substitute for the application of well- structured stress management or employee assistance programs (EAP), but rather to complement them. We should appreciate the value of EAP services, but there is also a significant value in pre-briefing. It makes the whole process more effective.

All of us need to develop mental and emotional muscles to effectively perform in extremely stressful and taxing times. Gary Mack, who is a sports psychologist, developed a concept called Mental Aspects of Performance (MAP). MAP teaches a basic set of skills designed to improve performance during routine times and under periods of increased stress. It is a set of learnable concepts and skills designed to help make us more effective. MAP concepts should be integrated into training programs. They should get periodic attention throughout a person's career. *Mental Aspects of Performance* is available through Fire Protection Publications at Oklahoma State University.

- **Standard Operating Procedures:** Another element that requires attention by the organization is developing and maintaining Standard Operating Procedures (SOPs). There is probably nothing that can more positively or negatively affect work outcomes and employee safety. Even when a full set of SOPs are in place, they are of little value if not used

35

regularly, critiqued, and kept current. The existence of SOPs directly affects safety and the quality of service delivered to our customers internally and externally. We must not lose sight of the target when it comes to the improvement of the safety and survival of our employees—and SOPs help us accomplish that.

- **Training and Development:** Having SOPs in writing and ensuring that everyone knows and uses them can be two different things. On-going skills training and performance evaluations are important to any organization. Basically, our members tend to play like they practice. We can have the greatest systems, SOPs, etc., in the world, but if we do not practice them regularly, we will not use them when specific situations arise. The lifeblood of any service organization is training. Our customers basically expect perfection. They expect us to perform well the first time...every time. This does not happen by chance. Basic skills training and other on-going training for new skills and knowledge must never be taken for granted in the organization. This training includes regular emphasis and follow-up on safety behaviors and SOPs. Positive, productive performance reviews and an active system for conducting various types and levels of performance critiques is a must for continuous improvement.

Another element of training is career development. Training programs must address today's needs and prepare employees for tomorrow. Educational growth should also be encouraged. Mentoring helps employees prepare for supervisory and management level positions. It is the responsibility of today's leaders to prepare tomorrow's leaders, and thus ensure the long-term effectiveness and success of the organization. It is not only our job to manage the organization today, but also to develop people in the organization to manage and lead tomorrow. This is one of the most important investments we can make in our organization's future.

Another component of career development is the ability to handle difficult situations or occurrences. Many people believe that non-routine times in an organization should simply be handled as natural escalations of the daily performance and system models that are in place. This task can be difficult for an organization to accomplish when there are no regular performance standards or regular system models (or SOPs) in place from which to escalate. In difficult times our members are not going to perform any better individually, or the organization collectively, than we do on a daily basis. We will always do better in tough times if what we are being expected to do seems to be a natural next step from what we do all the time.

Difficult challenges can be invaluable learning experiences for individuals and the organization as a whole. However, these challenges can also become very negative, divisive experiences. Some organizations and the careers of certain members simply do not survive these experiences. Difficult organizational times should not be taken lightly or just left to take their own course. It is a responsibility of leadership to guide the organization through these special times and help return the members to a sense of normalcy with regard to regular roles and the overall mission.

Transition to Retirement

With a little luck, a lot of willpower, patience, and guidance, most of us make it to the retirement phase of our careers.

Transitioning to the retirement phase should be an organizational concern and is, to some extent, considered a management responsibility.

- **Productive Employees:** Having the proper mindset going into retirement is very important. A critical piece of this mindset lies in being proud of one's performance during employment with the organization. This means that the members remain proud of their performance, and their fellow employees (and supervisors) remain proud of them as well. Irrespective of the rank a person holds, it is difficult to possess this pride or receive this respect when we are "coasting out" for the last few years we're on the job. When coasting, retiring persons do not usually feel very good about themselves, their work, or the organization. Their immediate supervisor and co-workers may develop resentment toward them. This is a very negative way to end a career, but we have all seen it happen. Even though we may be transitioning to retirement, this is not an excuse for a lack of effort or for incompetence. One way to avoid this organizational and personal trap is to instill in members the importance of always performing to the best of our ability, even up to, and including, the last day on the job. We will feel better about ourselves, and the people around us will have more positive feelings and memories about us as well.

- **Financial Stability:** Another element of retirement that deserves the organization's attention is monitoring pension and benefit packages to ensure that these plans provide adequate financial resources for a reasonable quality of life for retirees. The actuarial stability of pension plans is important. Paying a lot of organizational and individual attention to financial issues, including individual financial counseling, will help secure current and future retirees—then everybody wins.

Retirement transition doesn't just happen and can be a very stressful time in a person's life. Many people I know would either like to retire and cannot, or have retired without planning for it and are (in one way or another) unhappy with their decision to leave. Others, however, are very content retirees. Offering a retirement counseling program doesn't guarantee that retirement dissatisfaction and problems will not occur, but it is a step toward minimizing the frequency of such occurrences. A sound retirement planning program, started well ahead of departure, sets the stage for this significant change in one's life to be a positive step for the retiree—financially, and in every other way.

- **Appropriate Send-Off:** Members who retire should receive some form of appropriate send-off, even if it's a small gathering at the work site, and there should be at least one management representative present. The size of each retirement send-off may vary based on personalities and other factors. Organizations probably should not try to regulate that aspect. But it is a shame when a member retires and there is no opportunity for people to say good-bye, congratulations, or to thank them for their years of service. This is an important part of leaving and deserves some attention in the retirement process.

- **Employee Assistance and Medical Services:** It is hard to find an organization that has not experienced the benefit of offering Employee Assistance Programs (EAPs). However, perhaps we should take this a step further and continue to

39

provide access to these services for retirees and their spouses. Leaving the daily work life can present challenges for the retirees and their spouses. This is a significant change in one's life and can require help to navigate retirement and the aging process successfully. Not all retirees will take advantage of this opportunity, but many will. It makes good business sense to provide access to on-going personal, medical, and EAPs as employees transition to retirement. This can become part of standard retiree benefit packages if not already in place.

- **On-Going Contact:** On-going communication with retirees and opportunities for fellowship are other important pieces of a successful retirement. If there are department and/or union or association newsletters, they should be provided to retirees regularly. The organization can encourage retirees to attend social events, and perhaps even plan one specifically for the retirees periodically. It could be that there are volunteer jobs within the organization that retirees with certain skills can perform if they choose to do so. For some retirees, a complete break from the organization is their plan, but others find a sense of fellowship in continuing to be involved in some capacity. In some organizations (or with some people), this might be a good idea, and with others, maybe not. These are simply options worth considering that could keep the retirees more informed and enhance their self-esteem and sense of well being. If there were such options, members approaching retirement might feel that they could remain involved in some way, thus making retirement less traumatic.

As one can see, the organization's responsibility for the transition to retirement in a person's career is more than a final paycheck, a pen, a watch, a plaque, and a pension. If the organization viewed retirement as the final stage of a person's career, we might manage it differently and more effectively. We might begin to expand our view of what retirement can be for people who have devoted the majority of their adult work lives to the organization. Complete career management must include attention to retirement.

Conclusion

Career management as a component of effective human resource management does not happen by chance. There should be a plan, a programmatic approach to identifying critical success elements and implementing strategies to address them. Although not all-inclusive, the elements covered in this chapter are interrelated and require that each be in place to enhance their collective success. They provide a strong foundation from which to function. Some people believe that organizations should not view their management responsibilities this way anymore—that cradle-to-grave employment relationships are becoming a thing of the past. I challenge you to look around, because although this might be the case in some career fields, most of our fire service organizations are still hiring people for the long haul. Thus, we better manage their careers with that in mind.

Career management involves creating an overall process and environment designed to recruit and select the right candidates, get the absolute best from them everyday, and retire them healthy and stable (financially and otherwise). I hope this serves to stimulate thought, and helps provide direction for your organization.

A Few Things
about Change

Throughout time, leaders have been faced with the challenge of keeping organizations current and measuring their efficiency and effectiveness internally and externally. For fire service organizations, service quality is a key performance goal to define and measure.

Talking about improving things can be much easier than making improvements happen. Dealing with a lack of organizational patience, the on-going competition for scarce resources, and the natural human and physical resistance and barriers to change can take their toll on the best of leaders.

There are, however, some timeless guidelines that can help leaders move an organization to the future. These change-management "nuggets" have appeared for years in many of our readings. They are things others have told us, and some have come to us through experience (sometimes painfully). The following are a few of these nuggets that can serve to make the change process more effective:

- The most effective, widely embraced change is that which truly improves the core performance of the organization (inside. . . outside. . . or both). Core performance refers to the essence of the mission—the actual external service delivery or internal support improvements that are visible to the members.

- Change-for-change-sake can easily become this week's big deal. Without communication, focus, timing, and structure, resistance to change may significantly increase. People tend to resist constant attempts by others to "fix" them. Change packages do not need to be perfectly designed, but they do need to be perceived as thought-out and planned (to some extent) before they are presented and implemented.

- Communicate with, and nurture, those who are (or can become) key change leaders in the organization. They may then do the same for others within the system. This can improve positive support for improvements from within the organization. These key people may be formal or informal leaders. Win their support and commitment because many others will be inclined to follow their lead.

- The informal organization (positive or negative) can be as influential as the formal organization. Even if you cannot control this reality, do not forget or ignore it.

- Listen to those who disagree with a particular change. Sometimes resistance to change exists for good reasons that should be considered in the final decision. Disagreement is not necessarily negative. Listening to different points of view does not require agreement. It is actually a sign of strength by a leader.

- Ensure that new-hires and those who are newly-promoted buy into the mission and values of the organization. Value-based hiring and promotional practices have paid off for many organizations. They tend to match the person to the actual job requirements and to the organizational values. Then, if they possess the physical, emotional, and intellectual capability, they can be taught to perform their job duties.

44

- Participation in maintaining and improving one's own behavior and performance should not be optional. Nobody can expect to stay current in today's workplace without ongoing training designed to maintain basic skills and knowledge, as well as prepare for a changing future as job duties and organizational missions change.

- Creating and managing change requires skill, but it also requires enthusiasm and commitment from leadership. It also requires an active level of participation from the members. It is not possible to get others to consistently behave or perform in a particular way if the leaders are not willing or able to do so themselves. If the leadership cannot get excited about tomorrow or a new direction, then they should not expect the workforce to do so.

- Do not die trying to implement a specific change. The demise of a person's career is an organizational tragedy. Try not to take things personally. The idea is to keep coming back to lead again on other issues. Keep "showing up" and working to move the system toward strategic goals and a more effective tomorrow.

- It is difficult to **force** change upon the people who have to make the changes work. Attempting to exercise authority in this manner simply increases resistance and can create resentment between workers and managers. In the long run, change is more widely accepted when the workforce has the opportunity to participate in its development and implementation.

- Most people who get fed up do not get fed up and leave...they get fed up and stay. Programs designed to help the workforce stay positive, productive, and healthy will pay consistent dividends. Dissatisfied workers can have a negative impact on the mission and their co-workers.

- Leaders who are proponents of change cause people in the organization to be uncomfortable at times. Discomfort almost always accompanies significant change, no matter whose idea the change was. Significant change may be accompanied by the feeling of being out of control. It disrupts comfort zones in the workplace. Addressing these issues when planning change can help with implementation and enhance the success of the change.

- Leaders should spend some amount of time anticipating and planning for the future. Not only is this a simple, sound, management practice, but also it gives the workforce a constant preview of where the organization is headed.

- Have fun and help others do the same. This concept will help keep the organization moving forward. The workplace should not be a place where people hate to go. It does not have to be that way. We should, as leaders, make the workplace a positive place to be. People will perform more effectively when working in a positive, healthy work environment.

It can be useful to review some of the basics that tend to serve as anchor points for successful change. Those mentioned above can be helpful, and they will improve the effectiveness of change managers. Being aware of the challenges we face in our jobs and the reasons people act and react as they do will make us more capable of dealing with tomorrow.

Preparing Ourselves for a Changing Workplace

The following information is intended to assist individual employees (managers and workers) to deal more effectively with a changing workplace. The following are some very simple and time-tested concepts:

- External forces may drive change more than the internal environment; take advantage of opportunities that accompany change.

- Life's pace is faster, so we might have to accelerate ourselves (individually) to avoid being totally frustrated by the pace of the workplace.

- Be flexible, adaptable, and willing to change with the organization.

- Work today is not as structured. Do not expect to have your role explicitly defined by your supervisor.

- Sometimes it is easier to find joy in work when we periodically renew our personal commitment to our work.

- Provide quality service to internal and external customers. Always work on nurturing relationships throughout the workplace.

- Take responsibility for our own sense of well being. Recover faster from negative experiences and learn to let go of things from the past that tend to make us unhappy today.

- Accept responsibility and be accountable for our own behavior, performance, and results.

- Add a personal touch to our work. It can improve the quality of performance and add value to the organization.

- Be a lifetime student. Never assume we know it all. A "fully trained" mentality is the beginning of becoming obsolete.

- Avoid the inclination to blame. Emphasize ways to correct situations and go on to tomorrow and the new challenges it presents.

- Develop a keen sense of self-satisfaction for results, an active sense of humor, and a strong sense of loyalty to yourself and your own well being.

Five Additional Thoughts

1. Significant change will not usually occur by chance.

2. Change is most effective when couched and communicated within the context of the service delivery and support systems that exist in the organization.

3. Change sometimes has a lot of moving parts that someone has to round up and process for others who might be involved or impacted.

4. Significant change requires leadership, communication, involvement, system re-design (preferably written), resources, training, performance review, and system (as well as individual) feedback. It is a continual, dynamic loop.

5. It can take considerable time to institutionalize significant changes in system priorities and individual behavior or performance.

Change-Management Model

Utilizing a change-management model is very helpful in creating effective change. The following steps are an example one such model:

A. Identify the problem, challenge, or issue, as well as the parties or stakeholders who should be involved in the solution.

B. Develop alternative solutions and select one of them.

C. Identify and obtain necessary resources.

D. Develop a written plan and/or Standard Operating Procedure (SOP).

E. Provide information and training as necessary.

F. Implement the change (consider the timing).

G. Evaluate the success of the change. Listen to feedback.

H. Revise the plan or SOP if necessary.

I. Provide information and training on revisions as necessary.

J. Implement the changes, and so on, through this dynamic ongoing model.

Conclusion

The perfect formula for managing organizational change does not exist. The more we understand issues surrounding change and the reactions people tend to have to the process, the more effective we will be. There are organizations that have created a culture that is more acceptant and adaptable to change than others, therefore making change-elements more naturally internalized by the system. The contents of this chapter might help move your organization in that direction.

49

Neighborhood Oriented Fire and Rescue Services...An Element of Community Leadership

As part of the tradition of the fire service, fire stations in a community are integrated participants of neighborhoods. They were built as symbols of safety and protection. Firefighters and fire stations were viewed as the caretakers of the people and property in the neighborhood. They were also a place to go or someone to call when a person needed help, friends, or even counselors for adults and children. Firefighters were dedicated heroes, the ones who could always be counted on. Although this is still true, in some cities (or portions of cities), fire stations and firefighters now run the risk of being viewed differently. In fact, some fire stations are becoming fortresses designed to isolate the firefighters from the community they swore to serve. In some cities, stations might be locked down, perhaps so the public cannot have direct contact with the firefighters during the shift.

We frequently engage in conversations about "the basics." Discussions about how and why the fire service should return to the basics, and the importance of doing the basics well. Many times, these can be productive conversations because what is really being discussed is the importance of refocusing ourselves on the aspects of our service that are critical to our overall effectiveness, individually and collectively as organizations. Community involvement is one of those basics that needs additional focus in some of our fire departments. This vision of the future should include a snapshot from the past. Fire stations must integrate themselves within the neighborhoods in which they are located and must place a priority on being perceived as concerned participants who are interested in issues relating to the well being of the people with whom they reside. Community support for fire departments has traditionally been very high. Even so, in order to sustain this support, it is important that each fire department be committed to a long-term, fully integrated relationship with the community. There is a model that describes initial elements of an approach that would result in short and long term gains. The components of this model could apply to literally every community. What might differ is the extent to which each relates based upon the physical and social needs of a specific location or neighborhood. What is needed and might be effective in one neighborhood may not be a priority in another. Significant flexibility within the model will result in a more successful effort.

Commitment and Training

The entire leadership of the organization is responsible for developing and communicating the mission of the department and for defining and modeling the reason for the department's existence. This definition includes clearly describing how the members of the organization should deal with each other internally and interact with external customers. As a group, we are not going to interact much better with people outside the department than we do with each other inside the system. A truly integrated (community oriented) service delivery system must be cultivated from, and through, the members in the fire stations and other areas around the fire department. The focus of their efforts should be driven by their duties or directed within their first-due response areas, which is their neighborhoods of responsibility. This will require an empowering leadership approach that is modeled at the top and permeates throughout the organization. In order to grasp the full range of what might be included in such an effort, we may need to redefine expectations and develop a new set of skills and a broadened base of knowledge from which to operate. In order to accomplish this redefinition, a significant internal training package must be developed and delivered. This commitment to training should be ongoing because it, more than anything else, will drive the effectiveness of this community aligned system.

Potential Activities

What drives successful community involvement programs is simple. Every contact with the people in the community must be viewed by the members of the fire department as a moment of truth—an opportunity to serve, show that we care, deliver our message, and listen to the needs and perspectives of people. The only real limitation to defining these opportunities exists within our imaginations. For instance, in-service fire companies should be present at significant community activities that occur within their first-due areas. These might include special events, health fairs, and community/neighborhood meetings such as homeowners associations, block-watches, business groups, etc. The department's role would be to educate, listen, provide injury prevention materials, and develop and nurture a bond with the neighbors.

53

Providing blood pressure readings, immunization programs, and other minor health screening services at the fire station is also a meaningful service. Partnering with local businesses to periodically host an open house at the station and providing regular fire station tours (with a structured public education component) are other options. Interacting with local schools to serve as role models and mentors to children might be attractive to some fire department members. Some community fire stations have programs in which firefighters teach kids to read. Others have helped young people fill out job applications, and some tutor in areas such as practicing for job interviews. There are plenty of How-To guidelines already developed and available to fire departments. These guides address almost anything a station might want to do. There is no limit to what crews might develop by themselves if they are empowered and encouraged to do so. At the very least, the firefighters will learn more about the problems and opportunities that exist in the community, and they will get to know the people. Improved public information activities with the media, better all risk public education through programs such as the National Fire Protection Association's Risk Watch™ program (and the community alliances Risk Watch™ naturally creates), as well as the ability to gain better fire code compliance and built-in protection might be included in the accomplishments provided by this community oriented approach. Fire companies will find that their personal safety when working in the streets, could be significantly enhanced through these efforts. This neighborhood interaction may also decrease vandalism and theft at fire department facilities.

Conclusion

Bottom line: fire department members should share in the ownership of problems and issues that exist within their communities and neighborhoods. To adequately service their neighborhoods, firefighters might need the capability to more easily access the system (social services included) if they are to be successful delivering service in the future. Within the Department's capabilities, this would include having the flexibility, training, tools, resources, and the support needed to help all members be effective. Most of the activities I have mentioned in this chapter do not require a great deal of money to implement or sustain. What is necessary is the commitment of a certain amount of time, energy, and some financial support where possible. We know we cannot be all things to all people, and we probably should not create the organizational frustrations involved in trying to do so. That is not what the concept of Neighborhood Oriented Fire and Rescue Services is about. In fact, our activities should be, as much as possible, related to our mission, which in essence is providing a full range of prevention, public education, and emergency response services to our communities in a variety of ways.

Nothing will replace our need to treat people with respect and show them compassion. If we do not do this, we send the message that we do not care about them. Even in the most dangerous, high crime areas of our communities, most of the people who reside within them are as much victims of the violence in the neighborhood as the firefighters. A community's problems are also our problems. In all communities, and in all of their neighborhoods, we can better connect with the customers, enhance our image, and provide better service overall. We can

55

also improve the department's standing in the community and perhaps enhance our own personal safety. Neighborhood Oriented Fire and Rescue Services provide a look at what will be part of our future. Let's get started if you haven't already done so. In reality, community involvement by members of the fire department is really just a return to the basics. It is also an excellent way to display community leadership and instill community involvement as a core value of the organization.

A Few Final Thoughts

I'm very fortunate to have the opportunity to interact with so many fire service people throughout the country. Every day brings more information and guidance concerning general leadership, getting the most we can from our resources, and bringing focus to any group's efforts. This book is an attempt to pass along some of what people have unselfishly shared with me in a variety of ways over time.

One of the key roles of leadership is to position the people in the organization to be successful. This includes aspects of organizational design; general management; the selection, nurturing, and direction provided to people throughout their careers; providing a conduit to our customers; and tending to our own professional and personal needs.

Your responses to the following questions might provide a snapshot of areas that require some attention in your fire department.

Organizational Self-Assessment

- Does my department emphasize and teach elements of personal leadership at all levels of the organization? If so, how frequently and in what format?

- How is ethical decision-making and behavior taught and reinforced in my department?

- Do the leaders in my department consistently model the behavioral expectations they have of others? Do I?

- Are the basic programs within the Change-Management Model being addressed in some way in my department? Are program objectives defined and measured?

- Do all members of my fire department understand their role in the area of public education and community involvement? Is community interaction encouraged in the fire station and supported by management and labor leaders?

- Is most change a positive event in my department? Is there a commitment by our leadership to effective idea management and creating a work environment that embraces organizational and programmatic change?

- Do I periodically assess my own personal capabilities and commitment to a variety of leadership and management practices? If so, how will I know if I am becoming more effective?

No matter what role you currently have in your organization, the content of this book has a direct application to you. Your organization's overall success is totally dependent upon the collective efforts of all participants—and that includes every member.

Personal and organizational leadership is everyone's responsibility. We are in the fire service by choice, and we have an incredibly important role in society. Being at our best all the time must be a key goal for each of us, whether in prevention efforts, public education, emergency response, or any of the support areas that make delivering these services possible.

I hope you have found the information in this book interesting and useful. Thanks for investing your money and time to read it. I wish you the best as you proceed with your career. Take care and have fun.

About the Author

Dennis Compton is a well-known speaker and is the author of the *When In Doubt, Lead!* series, as well as many other articles and publications. His background includes a significant consulting and teaching history covering a wide variety of disciplines and subjects.

Dennis is the Fire Chief in Mesa, Arizona. He previously served as Assistant Fire Chief in the Phoenix, Arizona, Fire Department. During a career that spans almost thirty years, Chief Compton has been an active participant in the National Fire Service. As a result, many fire departments and other professional organizations have recognized his accomplishments. Among other affiliations, he is the Immediate Past-Chair of the Executive Board of the International Fire Service Training Association (IFSTA), and is the Vice-Chair of the Congressional Fire Services Institute's National Advisory Committee. Dennis is a charter member of the Arizona Fire Service Hall of Fame.

One colleague said, "Chief Compton has the unique ability to simplify typically complex organizational issues. Dennis has displayed this as an educator at colleges, universities, private corporations, and conferences throughout the country for many years.

His down to earth way of communicating frames a perspective that readers find refreshing and thought provoking. We know you will enjoy this latest effort."